100 CARS
THAT CHANGED THE WORLD

Publications International, Ltd.

Louis Weber, CEO
Publications International, Ltd.
8140 Lehigh Avenue
Morton Grove, IL 60053

Permission is never granted for commercial purposes.

ISBN: 978-1-64558-124-6

Manufactured in China.

8 7 6 5 4 3 2 1

CREDITS

We would like to thank the following vehicle owners and photographers for supplying the images for this book.

1912 Stutz: O: Craig Eicberg; P: Vince Manocchi. 1924 Packard: Ed and Judy Schoenthaler; P: Doug Mitchel. 1929 Duesenberg: O: Ray Scherr; P: Vince Manocchi. 1930 MG: O: John A. and Helen Heist; P: Doug Mitchel. 1932 Ford: O: Dave Gill; P: Vince Manocchi. 1934 Chrysler: O: Robert Hepler; P: Vince Manocchi. 1940 Jeep: O: Leonard C. Cassaro; P: Doug Mitchel. 1949 Cadillac: O: Steve Plunkett; P: Al Rogers. 1949 Ford: O: Gordon A. Fenner; P: David Temple. 1950 Nash: O: Warren Danz; P: Doug Mitchel. 1955 Chevrolet: O: Walter Lee Fogle; P: Doug Mitchel. 1961 Lincoln: O: Donald W. Wesemann; P: Doug Mitchel. 1962 Shelby Cobra: O: Richard Ellis; P: Al Rogers. 1964 Pontiac: O: Brian Thomason; P: Mike Spenner. 1965 Ford Mustang: O: Craig Chesley; P: David Temple. 1968 Dodge Charger: O: Douglas Lombardo; P: Doug Mitchel. 1968 Plymouth: O: Gary Schneider; P: Doug Mitchel. 1977 Chevrolet: O: Adam Wadecki; P: Nick Komic. 1980 AMC: O: Bill Harroun; P: Don Keefe. 1983 Ford: O: David A. Sevigny; P: Al Rogers.

Special thanks to the following manufacturers and organizations who supplied imagery.

Aston Martin Lagonda Limited, Barrett-Jackson, Bentley Motors Limited, BMW Group, Bugatti Automobiles S.A.S., Daimler AG, Ferrari S.p.A., Fiat Chrysler Automobiles, Ford Motor Company, General Motors Company, Honda Motor Co., Ltd., Jaguar Land Rover Limited, Lamborghini S.p.A., Mazda Motor Corporation, McLaren Automotive, Porsche AG, Toyota Motor Corporation, Volkswagen AG.

Additional imagery supplied by Shutterstock.com and Wiki Imagery.

TABLE OF CONTENTS

...ery story has to start somewhere, and for the automobile it is with the Benz Patent Motor Car. Carl Benz designed the very first car, and was granted a German patent in January 1886... ...e car was first driven in public on July 3, 1886, in Mannheim, Germany. Benz's three-wheeler was powered by a water-cooled single-cylinder engine, and had an estimated top speed o... ...kilometers per hour (9.9 mph). This simple car proved Carl Benz's ideas worked, and after improvements were incorporated about 25 examples of the Patent Motor Car were produced... ...d sold starting in 1888.

About the same time Carl Benz was working on his automobile in Mannheim, Gottlieb Daimler was pursuing the same general idea in Stuttgart, Germany. In 1884, Daimler and Wilhelm Maybach created the so-called "grandfather clock" engine, an upright single-cylinder, four-stroke design. The following year, a smaller version of the engine was installed in a two-wheeled "riding car" that actually looked more like a wooden bicycle. Daimler's "motorized carriage" of 1886 was the first four-wheeled automobile, and it was completed weeks after the Benz three wheeler made its public debut. Daimler's car was based on a horse-drawn carriage and was powered by a grandfather clock engine good for 1.1 horsepower.

1893 DURYEA

The 1893 Duryea is usually given credit as the first gasoline-powered American car. Brothers Charles and Frank Duryea installed a one-cylinder engine in a used buggy that was first driven on September 21, 1893 in Springfield, Massachusetts. A later Duryea won the first American automobile race that was sponsored by the *Chicago Times-Herald* newspaper and took place on a snowy Thanksgiving in 1895. The brothers formed the Duryea Motor Wagon Company in 1896 and commercially built 13 cars before the firm folded in 1898. Charles and Frank had a falling out and never worked together again.

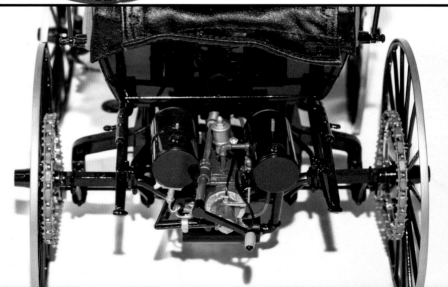

Emil Jellinek, an Austrian living in France, was an early automobile enthusiast and Daimler dealer. During 1900 Wilhelm Maybach designed a high-performance Daimler to Jellinek's wishes. The resulting 35-horsepower car was named after Jellinek's young daughter, Mercedes, and it was the automobile that helped move the young industry away from carriage-like design. The 1901 Daimler-Mercedes 35hp's basic layout proved trendsetting with its front-mounted engine, low hood, long wheelbase, and same-size wheels front and rear. Its four-cylinder engine featured many new design elements including camshaft-operated intake valves and a separate carburetor for each pair of cylinders.

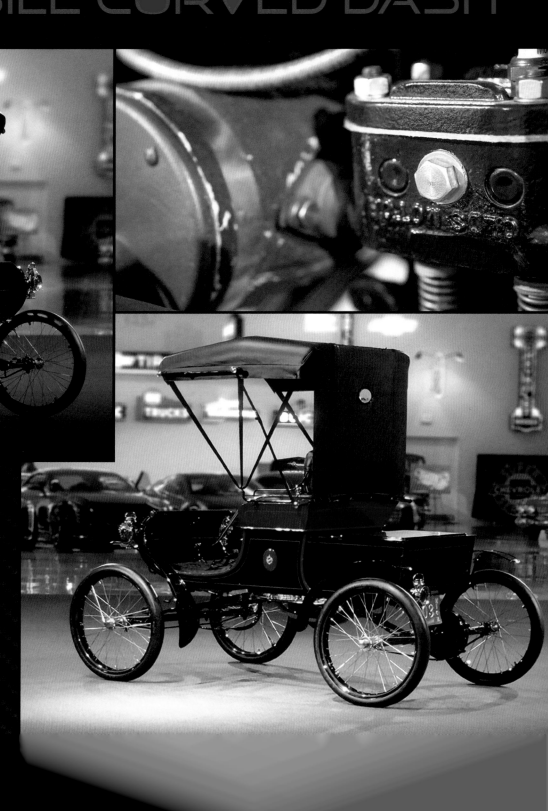

ne of the most important men in the early days of the automobile in merica was Ransom Olds. Though he had built some cars earlier, the 901 Oldsmobile Curved Dash runabout cemented his place in history. The mall, lightweight car was immediately recognizable thanks to the gracefully urved section at the front that inspired the car's name. A single-cylinder -horsepower engine was mounted under the two-passenger seat, and a ller was used for steering. Prices initially stated at $600, and production uickly ramped up from an estimated 425 cars in 1901 to 3924 in 1903. he Curved Dash Olds was once the best-selling car in America and the rst mass-produced automobile built on a stationary assembly line.

Rolls-Royce had built a number of models before it introduced the Silver Ghost for 1908. It was the Ghost that established Rolls Royce as a leading luxury make. The Silver Ghost was overengineered and overbuilt, which helped make it silent and reliable. It was powered by a 7-liter six that was later enlarged to 7.4 liters. With a light body, the Ghost was capable of around 80 mph. Wearing heavy armored bodies, the Silver Ghost proved its toughness in World War I, most famously with Lawrence of Arabia's guerrilla warfare in the Mideast. The Ghost remained in production until 1926.

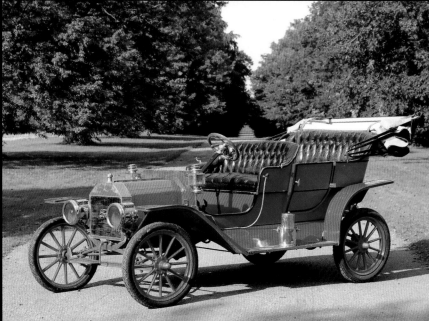

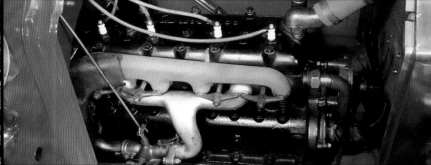

Today's Ford Motor Company was incorporated on June 16, 1903. On October 1, 1908, it introduced what may be the single most significant automobile, the Model T. It was known as the "Tin Lizzie," and Henry Ford's humble and utilitarian four-cylinder Model T proved responsible for popularizing the automobile. At first, the Model T only came as an open touring car priced at $825. More body styles were soon added, and as the moving assembly line helped dramatically increase production Ford reduced the price as low as $260 in 1924. Model T production ended in 1927 after more than 15 million had been built.

AN AMERICAN
TREASURE

1913 MERCER
TYPE 35-J RACEABOUT

Before the Ford-Chevy rivalry, there was Mercer versus Stutz. Both made American sports cars from before World War I into the mid-Twenties. The Mercer Raceabout was the lower, better handling of the two. In fact, respected auto writer Ken Purdy claimed ". . . a 1912 Mercer, on a winding road, twisty road, in the hands of a really good driver, can give a 1966 car a lot of trouble." The T-head Mercer Raceabout of 1911-14 was powered by a 58-horsepower four and had a top speed of around 75 mph. A later L-head Mercer was a little faster, but was heavier and less athletic. Production ended in 1925.

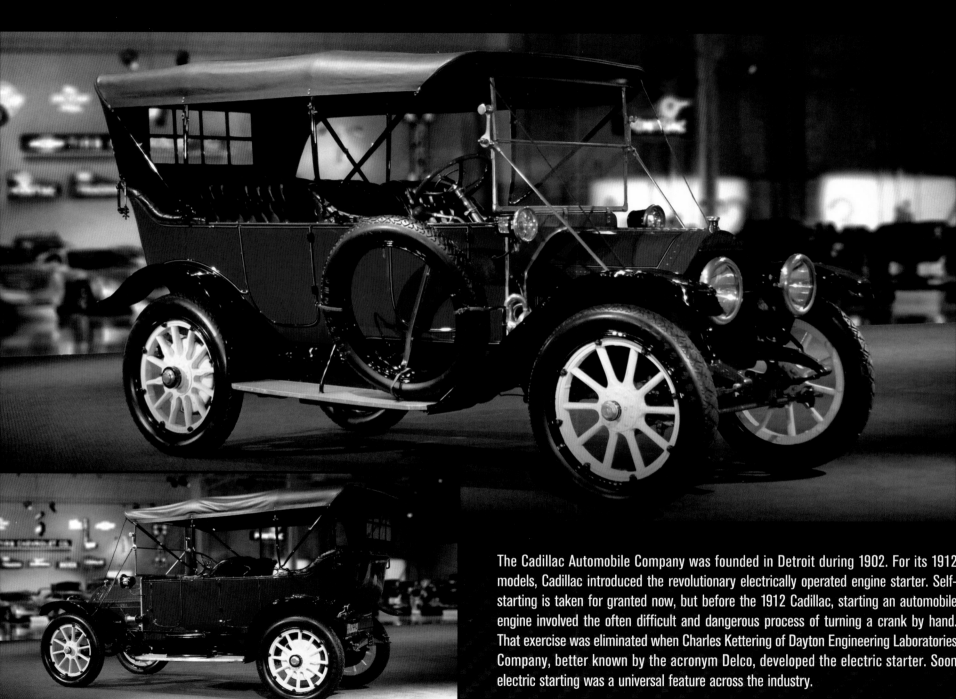

The Cadillac Automobile Company was founded in Detroit during 1902. For its 1912 models, Cadillac introduced the revolutionary electrically operated engine starter. Self-starting is taken for granted now, but before the 1912 Cadillac, starting an automobile engine involved the often difficult and dangerous process of turning a crank by hand. That exercise was eliminated when Charles Kettering of Dayton Engineering Laboratories Company, better known by the acronym Delco, developed the electric starter. Soon electric starting was a universal feature across the industry.

The Stutz Bearcat was born on a race track. The prototype's test drive was in the inaugural Indianapolis 500 in 1911 where it finished in 11th place and gained good publicity for the new make. The Bearcat was little more than bare chassis with 60-horsepower, 390-cid T-head four-cylinder engine and a minimum of bodywork. Top speed was around 75 mph. Although heavier, with inferior handling compared to its chief rival, the Mercer Raceabout, the rugged Stutz was better suited to the primitive roads of its time. Stutz had an impressive competition record and probably won more races than Mercer. Although the Bearcat was discontinued after 1924 (Stutz continued to sell other, less sporty, models), the sturdy Bearcat was a popular used car with college students throughout the Twenties. The Stutz company built its last car in 1934.

Cadillac's 1915 V-8 engine wasn't the first engine of its type in an automobile, but it was the first V-8 that entered mass production. Cadillac's original V-8 used a 90-degree layout, displaced 314 cubic inches, and was good for 70 horsepower. Depending on the body type, top speed reached as high as 65 miles per hour. The 1915 Cadillac V-8 five-passenger touring car started at $1975, which interestingly was exactly the same as the four-cylinder-powered 1914 Cadillac had cost.

1919 HISPANO-SUIZA H6

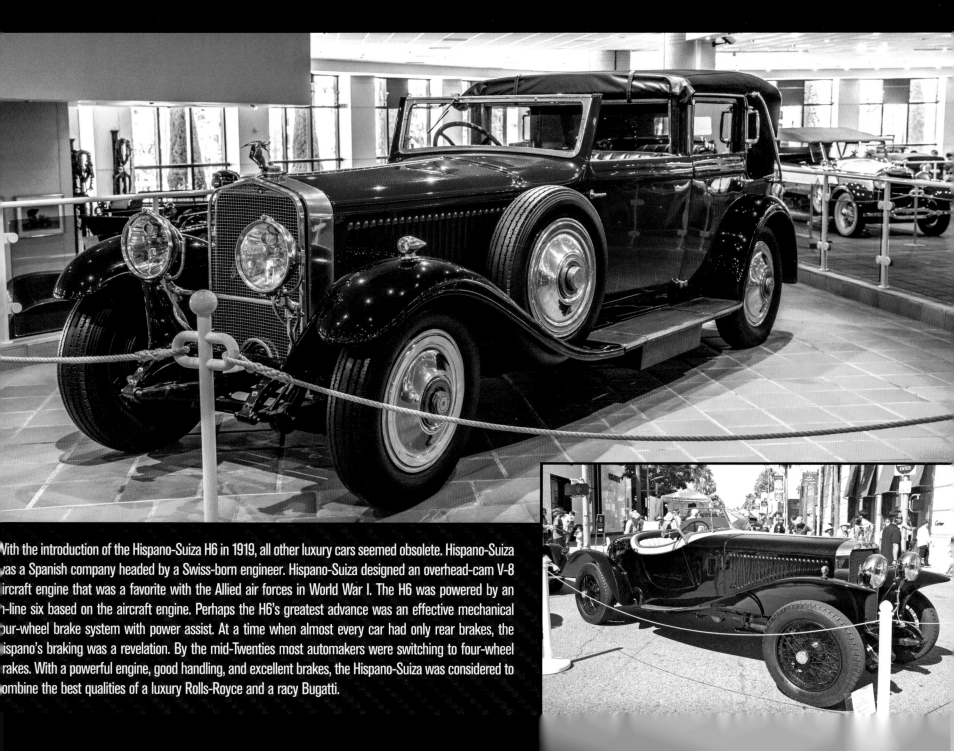

With the introduction of the Hispano-Suiza H6 in 1919, all other luxury cars seemed obsolete. Hispano-Suiza was a Spanish company headed by a Swiss-born engineer. Hispano-Suiza designed an overhead-cam V-8 aircraft engine that was a favorite with the Allied air forces in World War I. The H6 was powered by an in-line six based on the aircraft engine. Perhaps the H6's greatest advance was an effective mechanical four-wheel brake system with power assist. At a time when almost every car had only rear brakes, the Hispano's braking was a revelation. By the mid-Twenties most automakers were switching to four-wheel brakes. With a powerful engine, good handling, and excellent brakes, the Hispano-Suiza was considered to combine the best qualities of a luxury Rolls-Royce and a racy Bugatti.

The Duesenberg brothers, Fred and August, made a name in racing and introduced a luxury car for 1921. The Duesenberg Model A had America's first four-wheel hydrauli brakes–a system that would eventually be adopted by all makes. The engine was on of the first straight eights. This smooth-running layout would be popular in America cars from the Twenties into the early Fifties. The Model A engine featured an overhea camshaft and developed 100 horsepower. Although of advanced design and giving goo performance, the Duesenberg's conservative styling wasn't that special and sales of th expensive car suffered. The later Model J would make a much bigger splash.

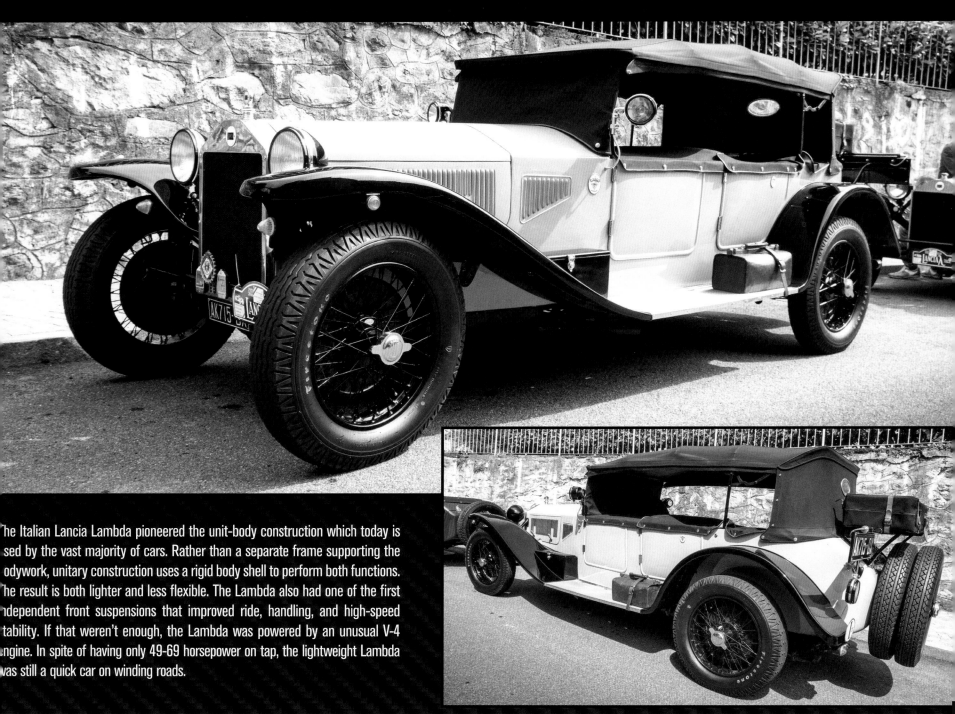

The Italian Lancia Lambda pioneered the unit-body construction which today is used by the vast majority of cars. Rather than a separate frame supporting the bodywork, unitary construction uses a rigid body shell to perform both functions. The result is both lighter and less flexible. The Lambda also had one of the first independent front suspensions that improved ride, handling, and high-speed stability. If that weren't enough, the Lambda was powered by an unusual V-4 engine. In spite of having only 49-69 horsepower on tap, the lightweight Lambda was still a quick car on winding roads.

In the years between the two World Wars, Bugatti enjoyed a reputatio similar to Ferrari today. The Type 35 cemented the French automaker' reputation. The Type 35's engine was overhead-cam straight eight wit three valves per cylinder. It was built in 2.0-liter and 2.3-liter capacitie in supercharged and non-supercharged versions with horsepowe ranging from 74 to 138. In cars that weighed less than a ton, the Typ 35 was capable of as much as 135 mph. Primarily a race car, the Typ 35 won over 1000 races in its career. An advanced feature of the Typ 35 was the use of lightweight aluminum-alloy wheels, perhaps the firs alloy wheels.

Packard was well established as one of America's leading luxury cars by the Teens. In 1924 Packard replaced its topline Twin Six (V-12) with a new straight eight–which was called "Single Eight" for its first year. The 85-horsepower eight helped make Packard the best-selling luxury car in the world. V-8s of the time had vibration periods, but Packard's straight eight with its nine-bearing crankshaft was extremely smooth running. Straight eights would be popular in luxury cars until World War II. Packards were engineered and built to high standards and were respected not just in America, but around the world. Packard built its last straight eight for 1954; by that time the most powerful version put out 212 hp. The car shown is a 1930 734 Speedster powered by a 145-hp straight eight.

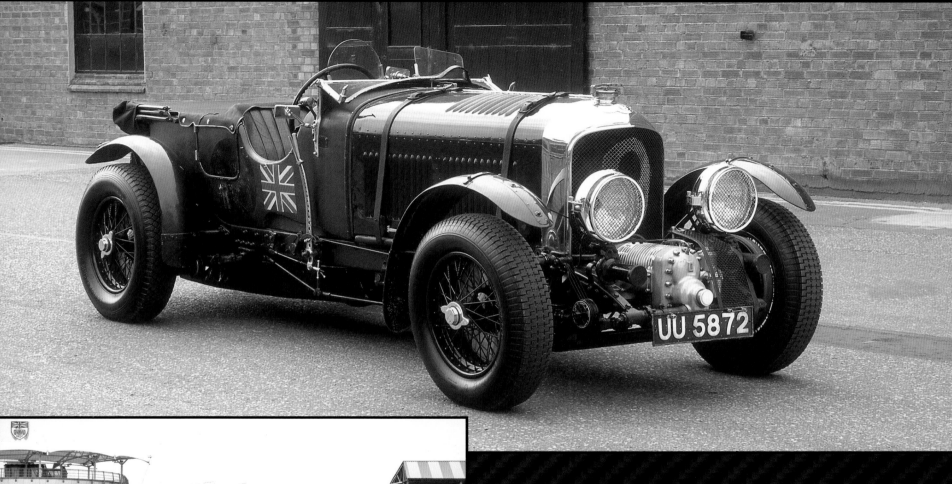

Bentley produced rugged English sports cars in the Twenties that inspired an enthusiastic following. The marque won five victories at Le Mans and Bentley was a source of national pride. The 4½ Liter was introduced for 1927. Its large, overhead-cam four-cylinder engine developed 110 horsepower. In pursuit of more power, a supercharged 4½ Liter or Blower 4½ (Blower is an English term for supercharger.) was added in 1929 and 50 were built to qualify for entry at Le Mans. Although the supercharger upped horsepower to 240 in racing versions, the Blower 4½ was never successful in racing. However, it's the most sought-after Bentley among collectors.

Daimler built the first production supercharged engine in 1923. Daimler merged with Benz in 1926 to produce Mercedes-Benz cars and in 1927 dropped the supercharged six in a sport touring chassis to create the S. The supercharger in the S was only engaged when the accelerator was floored and horsepower jumped from 120 to 180. The S was capable of more than 100 mph and spawned even faster cars. The 300-horsepower SSKL was intended primarily for racing and was capable of 146 mph.

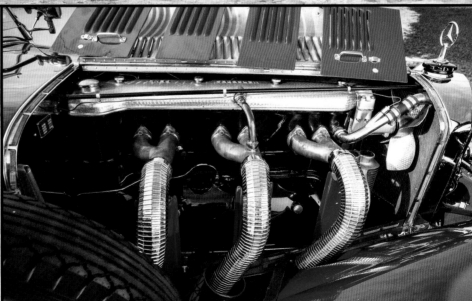

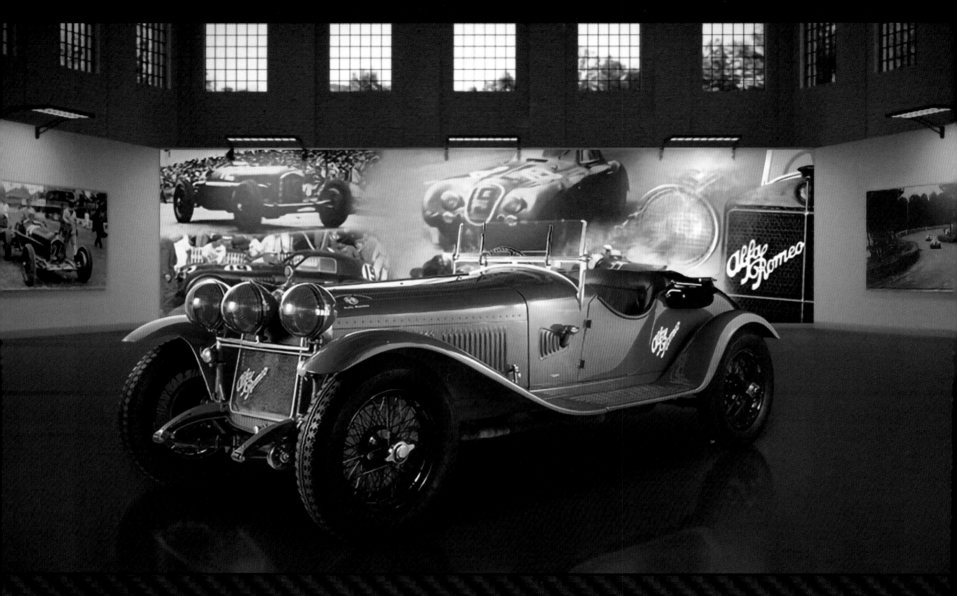

lfa Romeo was one of the top makes in European racing and the exotic sports car market in the Twenties and Thirties. The 6C had a banner year in 1929 winning the Mille Miglia, Belgian Grand Prix nd Monza Grand Prix. The 6C started out with an 1500cc six in 1927 but grew to 1750cc in 1929. The dual-overhead-cam engine was available with or without a supercharger. Horsepower ratings r 1750 version ranged from 46 to 85, with top speeds from 68 to 105 mph. Although the chassis was conventional for the time with beam axles and leaf springs at each end, the 6C was noted fo s excellent handling. Before Enzo Ferrari was famous for constructing his own race cars and sports cars, he got his start as a race car driver for Alfa Romeo in the Twenties and he managed Alfa'

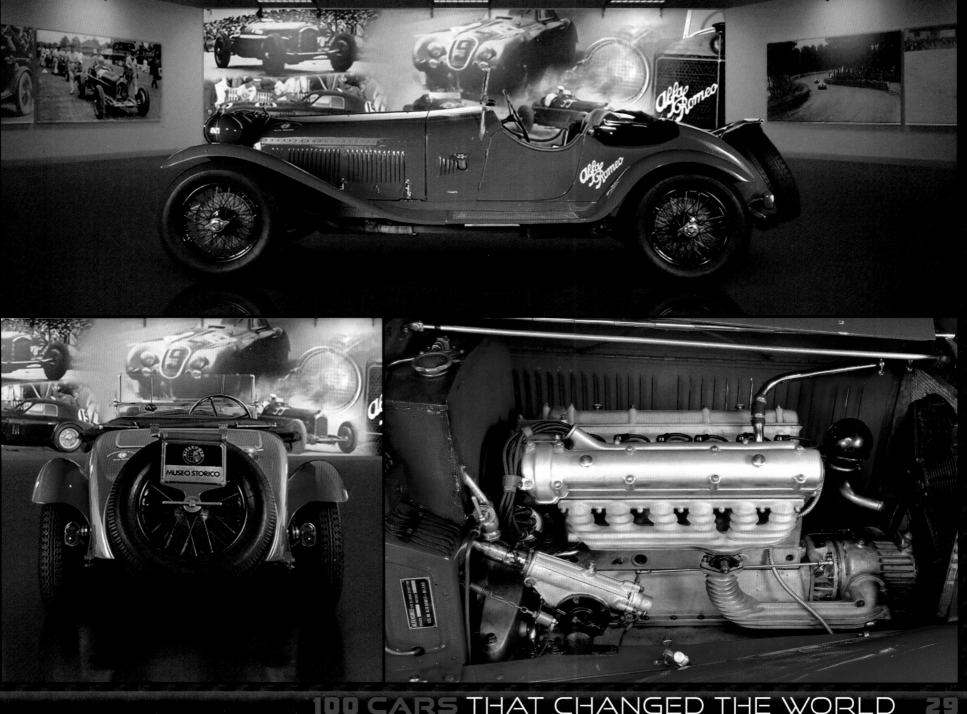

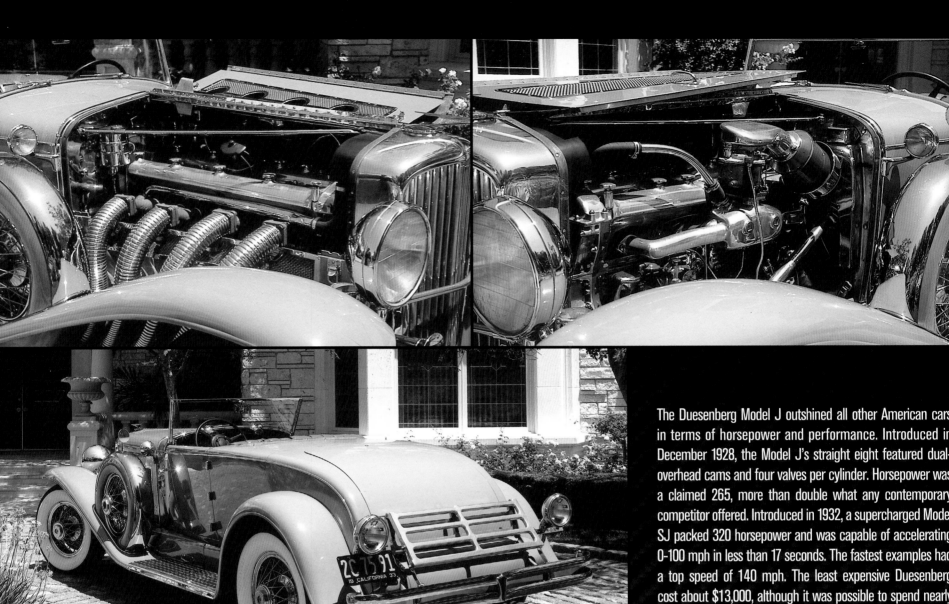

The Duesenberg Model J outshined all other American cars in terms of horsepower and performance. Introduced in December 1928, the Model J's straight eight featured dual-overhead cams and four valves per cylinder. Horsepower was a claimed 265, more than double what any contemporary competitor offered. Introduced in 1932, a supercharged Model SJ packed 320 horsepower and was capable of accelerating 0-100 mph in less than 17 seconds. The fastest examples had a top speed of 140 mph. The least expensive Duesenberg cost about $13,000, although it was possible to spend nearly double that on a Model J, though few did. When production finished in 1936, 470 chassis had been made.

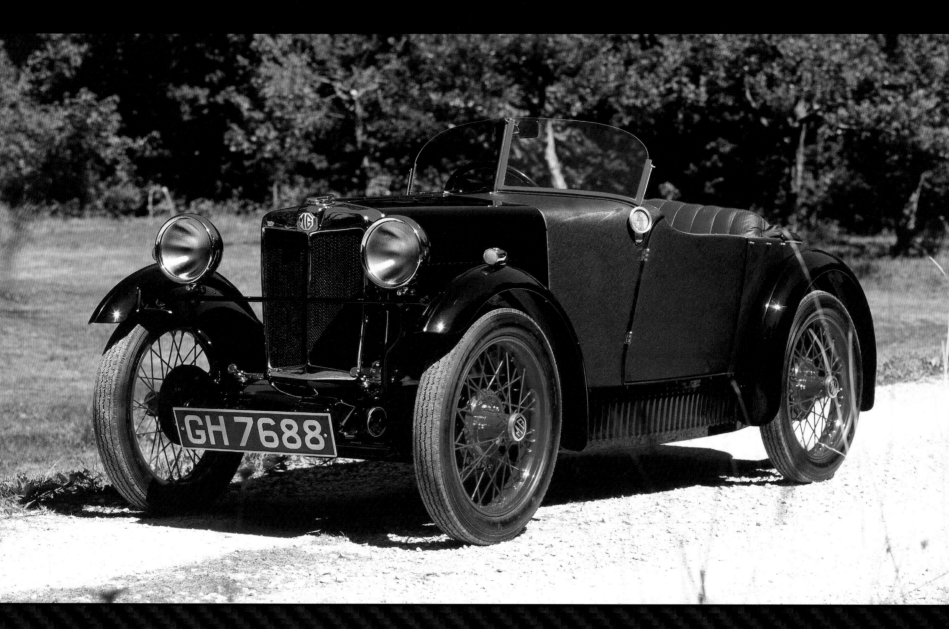

The MG M-Type Midget was the first of many low-priced MGs that introduced sports car ownership to greater numbers. The Midget followed a popular formula of using sedan components a the basis of a sports car. The M-Type combined a modified Morris Minor chassis with a Wolseley overhead-cam 4-cylinder engine and clothed it in a lightweight body. The result was chea and fun to drive. MG was the most popular sports car for many years.

Rolls-Royce built its reputation on the Silver Ghost, but
was decidedly dated after World War I. The Phantom I
1925 dropped a new overhead-valve six-cylinder engine i
the old Ghost chassis, but it was Phantom II introduced i
1929 that was really a new car. With a lower chassis an
a long hood, the Phantom II showed custom coachwor
to its best advantage. Besides the stately limousines an
sedans, there was also a short Continental chassis fo
high-speed touring that was capable of exceeding 90 mph

As America plunged into the Great Depression, Cadillac introduced its magnificent Series 452 V-16 models for 1930. The V-16 caught the industry by surprise, and it powered new top-of-the-line Cadillacs that competed with the handful of true luxury brands at the absolute high end of the market. Designed by Owen Nacker, the beautifully finished engine displaced 452 cubic inches. It was good for 165 horsepower and an impressive 320 lb-ft of torque. A wide variety of body styles were offered. Prices covered a spread from $5350 for the two-passenger roadster to $9700 for the town brougham. Production for 1930 and '31 combined was 3250 units.

Ford's legendary "flathead" V-8 engine made its debut on March 31, 1932. The 221-cubic-inch engine was good for 65 horsepower. It broke technological ground by using an engine block cast as a single piece, and was the first V-8 engine available in a low-priced car. Ford's 1932 Model 18 V-8 wore clean styling that masterfully evolved from the 1930-'31 Model A's appearance, and the most basic two-seat V-8 roadster listed for $460. A four-cylinder-powered Model B looked almost exactly the same and cost $50 less. More streamlined styling was introduced for 1933 and the Ford's appearance was updated yearly. A 1936 model is shown here.

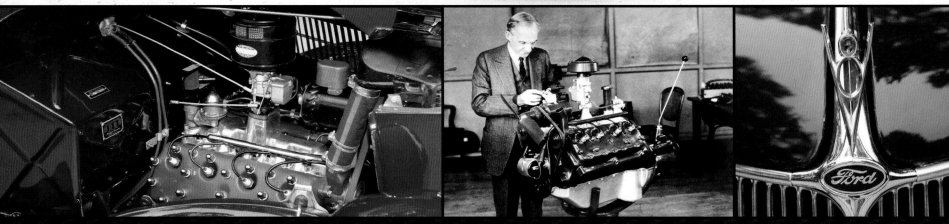

Any list of great American luxury automobile brands has to include Pierce-Arrow. Pierce-Arrow was based in Buffalo, New York, and entered the automobile business in 1901. Studebaker purchased the company in 1928, but operations remained in Buffalo. Already wounded by the Depression, Pierce introduced new top-of-the-line V-12 models for 1932. At the 1933 Chicago World's Fair, the Silver Arrow debuted. The futuristic four-door sedan wore a dramatically Vee'd radiator, flush front fenders, had a radically tapered rear end, and lacked the era's expected running boards. It was powered by a 175-horsepower version of Pierce's V-12. The Silver Arrow's styling was at least 10 years ahead of its time, but the price was $10,000, and only five were built. The last Pierce-Arrows were the 1938 models.

The Chrysler Airflow failed to make money, but it did change the course of automotive design. Chrysler engineers knew that good aerodynamics could increase speed and fuel economy while reducing noise. The Airflow was introduced in 1934 with a wind-cheating body that functioned as promised, but didn't sell well because the public was turned off by its styling. Chrysler added a more prominent grille for '35, but the Airflow still didn't move and the 1937 model shown here was the end of the line. Aerodynamics became increasingly important in car design and are especially vital today. Another Airflow innovation was moving the engine forward over the front axle and placing the back seat ahead of the rear axle, which gave better interior room and improved ride. This feature was quickly copied by other makes.

Auburn, named after its Indiana hometown, dated to 1903. Erret Lobban Cord assumed control of the company in 1924. He decided Auburn needed an attention-grabbing car, which resulted in a series of Speedsters from 1928. The 1935 Auburn Speedster was the third such model, and it was a masterful creation designed by Gordon Buehrig on a shoestring budget. The center section of leftover 1931-'33 Speedster bodies were adapted to the 1935 chassis and front sheet metal, and the beautiful result was fitted with a supercharged 279.9-cubic-inch straight eight good for 150 horsepower. Performance was impressive for the day with a guaranteed top speed of 100 mph. Prices started at $2245. A 1936 model is shown.

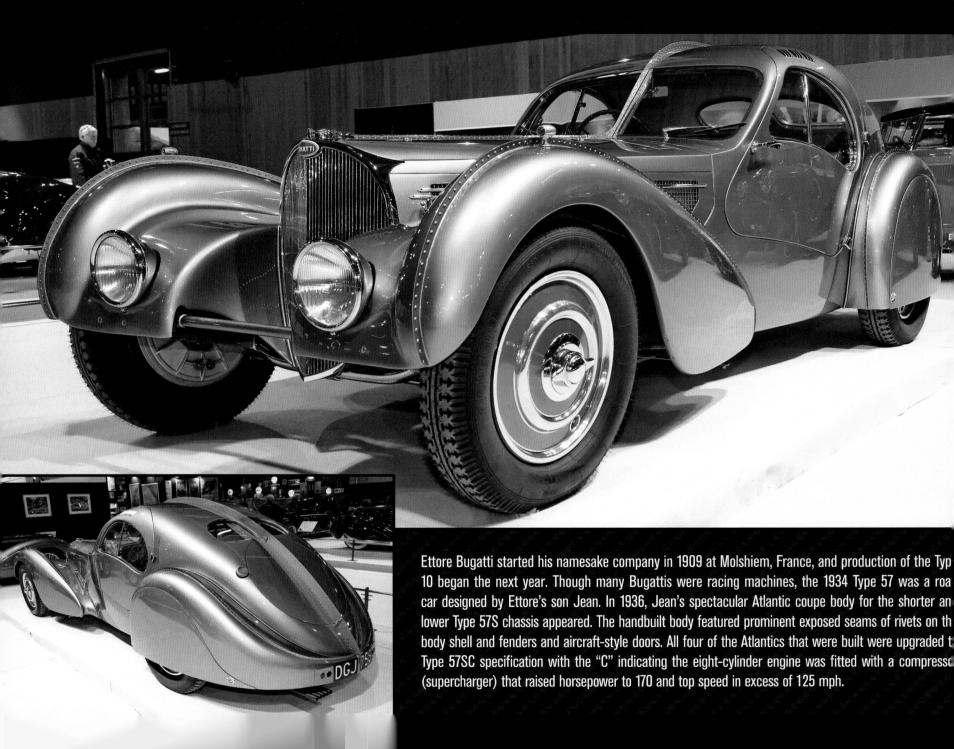

Ettore Bugatti started his namesake company in 1909 at Molshiem, France, and production of the Typ 10 began the next year. Though many Bugattis were racing machines, the 1934 Type 57 was a roa car designed by Ettore's son Jean. In 1936, Jean's spectacular Atlantic coupe body for the shorter an lower Type 57S chassis appeared. The handbuilt body featured prominent exposed seams of rivets on th body shell and fenders and aircraft-style doors. All four of the Atlantics that were built were upgraded t Type 57SC specification with the "C" indicating the eight-cylinder engine was fitted with a compresso (supercharger) that raised horsepower to 170 and top speed in excess of 125 mph.

Errett Lobban Cord was a "wheeler-dealer" who by the late 1920s owned the Auburn and Duesenberg car companies along with several other businesses. He added a front-wheel-drive car bearing his name in 1929. The Cord brand was inactive from 1933-1935, but for 1936 it returned with the magnificently styled 810. Appearance was striking with highlights including a "coffin-nose" hood and the industry's first hidden headlamps. Unusual for the time, it was again front-wheel-drive design and used unit-body construction. The engine was a Lycoming-built V-8 good for 125 horsepower in standard tune. For the 1937 812 models, an optional supercharger raised output to 190 horsepower. The supercharged Cord could accelerate 0-60 mph in 13 seconds and had a top speed of 110 mph. Sadly, Cord didn't make it past 1937.

The 1938 Buick Y-Job is generally accepted as the automobile industry's original concept car. General Motors's first design chief, Harley Earl, was the man ultimately responsible for the dramatic machine, and he was known to drive the Y-Job around Detroit. The long-and-low two-passenger roadster was built on a 1937 Buick chassis and wasn't intended to be a production model, but rather it was meant to be a "car of the future" that showcased new ideas that would later be found on production vehicles. These innovations included power windows, hidden door hinges, flush-mount door handles, and a convertible top that was hidden from view when lowered. Later Buicks picked up some the Y-Job's styling elements.

1·949

SMART VOLKS WORKS

The Volkswagen Type 1 started as a plan by Adolf Hitler's National Socialist party to create a "German people's car." Popularly known as the Volkswagen Beetle, this clever design by Ferdinand Porsch featured a platform chassis and a rear-mounted air-cooled "flat four-cylinder engine. In 1938 construction began on the massiv factory that would build the Beetle in today's city of Wolfsburg. Onl 630 Beetles had been produced by time the plant came under contro of the British military in 1945. Assembly restarted in December 1945 and when production concluded in 2003 at VW's factory in Puebla Mexico, more than 21.5 million Beetles had been built.

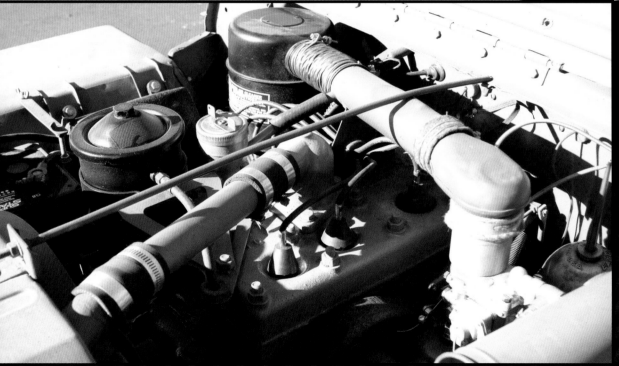

In the summer of 1940, American-Bantam, Ford, and Willys-Overland prepared prototypes as the companies compete to the supply the United States military with a new "ligh reconnaissance vehicle." The Willys design was eventuall chosen, and it's the vehicle that became famously known a the "Jeep." Features included a four-cylinder engine, four wheel drive, bodyside cutouts for quick entry and exit, and fold-down windshield. Willys-Overland manufactured almos 360,000 Jeeps for the war effort, and Ford Motor Compan built about 227,000 more to the Willys design. After the wa Willys trademarked the Jeep name, and the first "civilian Jeep, the CJ-2A, entered production in late 1945.

The MG TC helped spearhead the postwar sports car invasion in America. Legend has it that American service men stationed in England were exposed to sports cars. By the Forties, American cars had grown big and comfort was the priority. Although hard riding and not very fast (top speed 78 mph), the TC was a joy to drive with quick reflexes and good cornering. It was also affordable with a base price under $1900. The TC was a continuation of a mid-Thirties design and to American eyes seemed extremely old fashioned. Front suspension was a solid axle on leaf springs. The 1.3-liter overhead-valve four-cylinder engine was rated at only 54 horsepower, but the car weighed just 1735 pounds. The MG TD replaced the TC in 1950 and sold in much

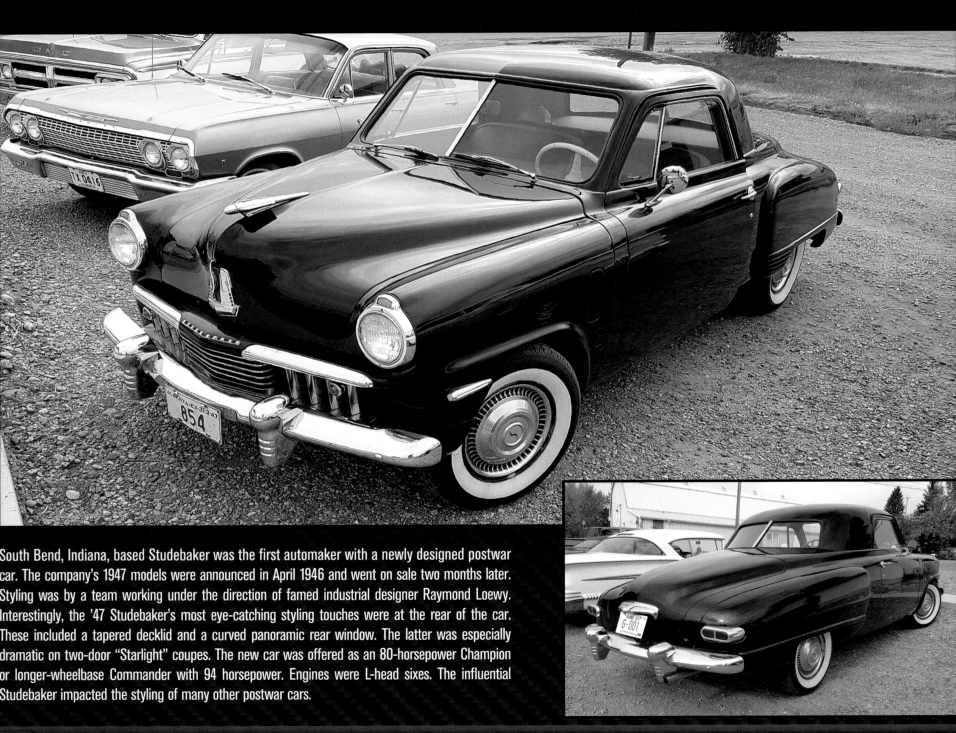

1947 STUDEBAKER

South Bend, Indiana, based Studebaker was the first automaker with a newly designed postwar car. The company's 1947 models were announced in April 1946 and went on sale two months later. Styling was by a team working under the direction of famed industrial designer Raymond Loewy. Interestingly, the '47 Studebaker's most eye-catching styling touches were at the rear of the car. These included a tapered decklid and a curved panoramic rear window. The latter was especially dramatic on two-door "Starlight" coupes. The new car was offered as an 80-horsepower Champion or longer-wheelbase Commander with 94 horsepower. Engines were L-head sixes. The influential Studebaker impacted the styling of many other postwar cars.

f the French Citroën 2CV looks like a Volkswagen Beetle with a thyroid condition, it might be because both cars were developed as a "people's car" just before World War II. The 2CV was set o debut just as Hitler invaded Poland, so the introduction had to be delayed until 1948. One of the engineer's goals was a car that could carry a basket of eggs over a plowed field without reaking an egg. With soft suspension and long wheel travel, the 2CV did have a smooth ride. The engine was a 9-horsepower 375cc 2-cylinder that gave a top speed of only 40 mph. The ngine eventually increased to 602cc and top speed reached 71 mph. The 2CV succeeded in its goal of providing economical transportation and was a familiar sight on French roads for many ears. In fact, the car had a production run of 42 years with the last 2CV produced in Portugal in 1990.

Ford's first redesigned postwar vehicle was the 1948 F-Series truck line that introduce the F-Series name that is still in use today. Available models ranged from the ½-ton F-1 a the way through F-8 for three-ton "extra" heavy-duty workhorses. The designers paid extr attention to the cab, which was taller and wider than the previous truck's, had bigger doc openings, and room for the driver and two passengers. The popular F-1 pickups had a be that was 6½ feet long. F-1 buyers could choose between a 226-cubic-inch inline six rate at 95 horsepower or the 239-cube "flathead" V-8 that was good for 100 horses.

While other makes mounted the floor on top of the chassis rails, the 1948 Hudson welded the floor under the chassis. This resulted in a lower car, without compromising ground clearanc or headroom. Passengers stepped down when entering a Hudson and 1948-54 Hudsons are commonly called "Step-downs". The lower center of gravity was a boon to handling. Hudso dominated NASCAR racing in the early Fifties, not because it had the most power, but because it could out-corner the other cars. Hudson faded away in the Fifties, but the step-down layou became the norm.

Jaguar developed a dual-overhead-camshaft six-cylinder engine after World War II. Previously, only race cars and exotics such as Duesenberg, Bugatti, and Alfa Romeo had used such a valvetrain. In order to ramp up production of its new XK engine before volume use in sedans, the first car to get the powerplant was the XK120 sports car introduced at the 1948 London Motor Show. The XK120 was based on a shortened sedan chassis with a new torsion-bar independent front suspension. The XK120 proved that a sports car could ride comfortably and still have good handling. The XK120 was named for its top speed and the car could exceed that figure—making the Jaguar faster than many competitors that cost much more.

The first Land Rover was introduced in 1948. Due to Britain's postwar austerity, automakers had to export a large portion of production to get rationed steel. The Rover car didn't have much export potential, but a Jeep-like 4-wheel-drive Land Rover prototype did. It had a simple but rugged frame and mechanicals. An aluminum body reduced the use of rationed steel. Britain's colonies and former colonies loved it. Soon, Land Rovers were traversing Africa and anywhere else where paved roads were rare. At one time, it was claimed that for a third of the world's population, a Land Rover was the first vehicle ever seen.

Cadillac debuted its first newly designed postwar cars for 1948, and their smart styling introduced the tailfin—which was copied by many other makes in the Fifties. Cadillac's otherwise largely unchanged 1949 models boasted two more trend-setting features. Most noteworthy was Cadillac's overhead-valve, short-stroke V-8 engine, a 331-cubic-inch job rated at 160 horsepower. The new engine weighed almost 200 pounds less than the L-head V-8 it replaced yet was more powerful. The overhead-valve V-8 went on to become the most popular engine type in American cars from the mid-Fifties through the Seventies. The 1949 Cadillac Coupe de Ville, along with the similar-in-concept Buick Roadmaster Riviera and Oldsmobile 98 Holiday, introduced hardtop styling. The hardtop gave the open feeling of a convertible with the windows down, while still providing the practicality and all-weather construction of a closed car. Shown is Cadillac's concept car that previewed its production Coupe de Ville.

Ford's first new postwar car debuted in June 1948, and it was the company's most thoroughly redesigned automobile since the 1928 Model A. The 1949 Ford exterior featured modern flush fender styling along with a prominent "bullet nose" ornament centered in the chrome grille. Underneath, the traditional "buggy spring" suspension and torque-tube drive preferred by Henry Ford were retired. In their place, an independent suspension was used up front, and out back parallel leaf springs carried a rear axle with Hotchkiss drive. The engines were Ford's familiar 226-cubic-inch straight six and 239-cubic-inch V8. The new Ford proved very popular, and production topped 1,118,000 units for the extra-long model year.

The 1950 Nash Rambler was the first "compact" car to find success in the American market. When production started at Nash's Kenosha, Wisconsin plant in February 1950 the only model was the 100-inch wheelbase Custom Landau convertible. The convertible's fixed side window frames were an unusual design choice. In June 1950, the ragtop was joined by an all-steel two-door station wagon also in Custom trim on a 100-inch span. The only engine was Nash's 82-horsepower L-head six. These Ramblers were small cars, but not cheap cars. Both models were nicely equipped, and cost $1808 to start. First-year production was 11,042 units, but in '51 the tally rose to 68,762. The car shown has Rambler's new for '53 styling.

The 1951 Chryslers were modestly facelifted versions of the 1949 models. But there was big news under the hood in the form of Chrysler's first V-8 engine. Called the FirePower, it was the company's first "Hemi." The new engine followed big bore and short stroke design principles, but the cylinder heads diverged from the expected and used hemispherical combustion chambers with angled intake and exhaust valves set to either side. This design allowed for a centrally mounted spark plug, which resulted in more efficient combustion and helped the engine produce 180 horsepower from 331 cubic inches. Tradeoffs included cylinder head complexity and weight, along with increased production costs.

With Bentley becoming more like its corporate sibling, Rolls-Royce, the R-Type Continental was a return to Bentley's sporting heritage. Bentley's 4.6-liter 6-cylinder engine was tuned to produce more power and a streamlined, lightweight coupe body was designed for the car. High-speed touring was the goal of the Continental and it was one of the fastest cars in the world with a top speed of 115 mph and a cruising speed of 100. Today, the R-Type Continental is one of the most collectible of postwar Bentleys.

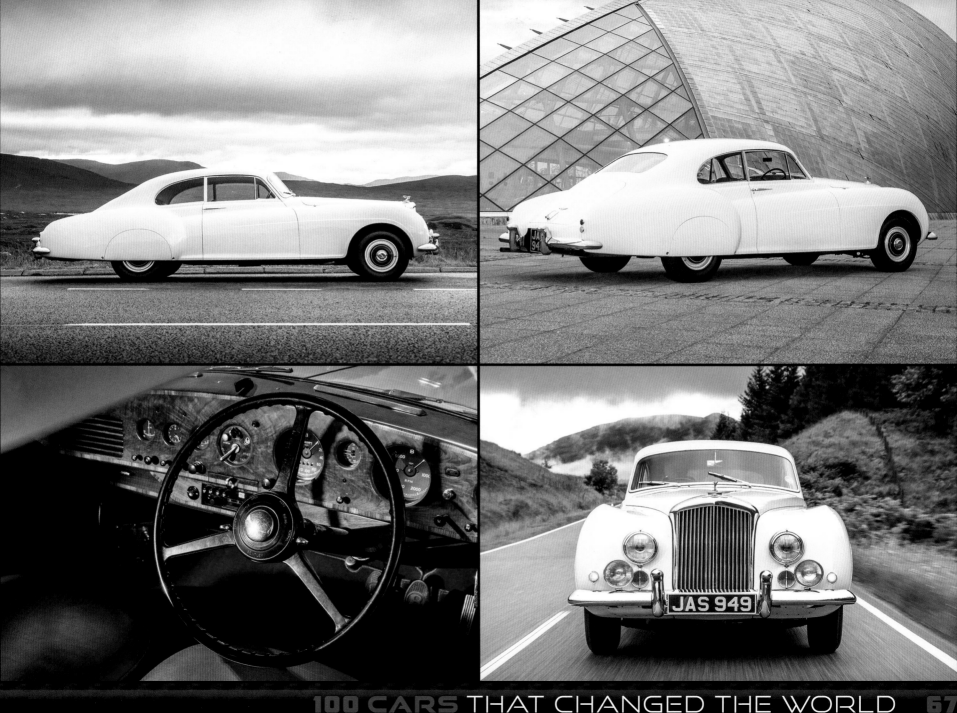

In early 1953 Chevrolet introduced the two-seat Corvette at that year's GM Motorama. On June 30th, Corvette entered limited production, and its appearance varied little from the show car. Highlights included molded-fiberglass convertible bodywork, a chrome-framed wraparound windshield, and wire-mesh stone guards over recessed headlamps. A folding top and plastic side curtains added protection in bad weather. While the styling screamed "sports car," the powertrain disappointed. A Corvette-specific version of Chevy's "Stovebolt" six included three carburetors and was good for 150 horsepower, but it was only available with the two-speed Powerglide automatic. Just 315 of the '53 Corvettes were built. All were Polo White with Sportsman Red interiors.

The 1954 Mercedes-Benz 300SL "Gullwing" coupe traces back to a 1952 M-B racing car of the same name. Max Hoffman, the Mercedes-Benz importer on America's East Coast, convinced the German company a road-going 300SL would sell and the production version made a New York City debut in February 1954. The car's defining feature was the so-called gullwing doors, which opened upward and included large sections of the roof. This design was necessary because the car's elaborate tube frame took up much of the space needed for conventional doors. The 300SL's six-cylinder was the first production fuel-injected gasoline engine. Prices started around $7500, and about 1400 cars were produced.

1955 CHEVROLET V-8

The 1955 Chevrolet had attractive new styling with a wraparound windshield, smooth bodysides, and a simple Ferrari-inspired grille. The big news was under the hood, Chevy's new 265-cubic-inch V-8. A clean-sheet overhead-valve design, the Chevy V-8 weighed less than the old Chevy "Stovebolt" six, but was more powerful. Standard versions were good for 162 horsepower with manual transmission or 170 with Powerglide automatic. The optional Power-Pak added a four-barrel carburetor and dual exhaust for 180 ponies. Chevrolet's new V-8 would become legendary as the "small block". Chevrolet moved more than 1.7 million of the '55s, a new record for the brand. A gold '55 Chevy Bel Air Sport Coupe was celebrated as the 50-millionth car built by General Motors.

1957 CHRYSLER

Chrysler Corporation's 1957 line was a revelation. Virgil Exner's styling was lower and sleeker than the competition. Plus, there was new torsion-bar front suspension that improved handling without sacrificing ride. Often under the hood was the corporation's Hemi V-8. Unfortunately, the '57s were developed quickly and customers encountered quality issues. The 300-C was Chrysler's halo car. It was a well-equipped hardtop coupe or convertible with a 392-cid Hemi V-8 that was rated at 375 horsepower or 390-hp for an optional version that was recommended for competition use only. With the standard engine, the 300-C was capable of accelerating 0-60 mph in 8.4 seconds.

The 1955 Ford Thunderbird was Ford's response to Chevrolet's 1953 Corvette. Like the Chevy, the T-Bird was a two-seater, but it had a steel body, was more luxurious, and didn't suffer from as many compromises as the sportier Vette. Ford switched strategy and introduced a larger and more luxurious four-seat Thunderbird for 1958, and it sold much better than the earlier model. Available as a convertible or hardtop, the '58 T-Bird used unibody construction and was powered by a 352-cubic-inch V-8 good for 300 horsepower. The interior included a new control console mounted on top of the transmission tunnel, a feature that remains widely popular today. The four-seat Thunderbird helped popularize the "personal luxury" car.

1959 BMC MINI

The 1959 BMC Mini was one of the most influential cars of the twentieth century. Built in response to a brief European energy crisis in 1956, the Mini was designed by visionary engineer Alec Issigonis to give the maximum amount of passenger space in a small package. Its transverse engine, front-wheel-drive layout became the small car norm by the Eighties. The product of British Motor Corporation, Minis were sold with Austin, Morris, Riley, Innocenti, and Wolseley badges. Minis became fashionable in the Swinging Sixties and that popularity was increased by the racing and rally success of the sporty Mini Coopers. The basic Mini design was produced until 2000.

Colin Chapman shook up the racing world with his Lotus race cars and his first road car was also revolutionary. The 1959 Lotus Elite was the first car with fiberglass monocoque structure. Very little structural steel was used in the car. The result was a car that weighed only 1450 pounds. The tiny 1216cc Coventry-Climax overhead-cam four-cylinder engine cranked out only 83 horsepower, yet the top speed was 118 mph. The Elite also had four-wheel independent suspension and four-wheel disc brakes. Handling was a revelation at the time. However, the car was loud and had poor ventilation. Plus, Lotus lost money on every car they sold. Lotus introduced the more successful Elan in 1962 and phased out the Elite in 1963.

1960 FERRARI 250 GT SWB

The Ferrari 250 GT Spyder California originated with a request by a West Coast Ferrari distributor for a fast convertible for 1957. Styling was by Pinin Farina and 50 were built. A second-generation California on a shorter wheelbase entered production in 1960. A 280-horsepower V-12 was under the low hood and the California was advertised as "ready to race," but few owners did. Only 56 SWB versions were built before production ended in 1963. The California is considered one of the most beautiful and collectible Ferraris. The California's gorgeous looks landed it a role in the 1986 film *Ferris Bueller's Day Off*, although replicas were used instead of a multi-million-dollar original.

The Jaguar E-Type (XKE in US advertising) created a sensation when it debuted at the 1961 Geneva International Motor Show. The semi-unitized construction was based on Jaguar's D-Type race cars and the 265-horsepower dual-overhead-cam six was carried over from the XK150. Its new independent rear suspension would serve Jaguar for many years. The styling regularly makes top ten lists for most beautiful cars. The car could accelerate 0-60 mph in less than seven seconds and reach a top speed of 150. The initial price was less than $6000–a fraction of the price of cars with similar performance. The E-type gained a V-12 engine in 1971 and the last models were sold in 1975.

In the late Fifties, Lincolns were huge cars with flamboyant styling. Sales were disappointing. Lincoln decided that a sensibly-sized luxury car with simple, classic styling would revive the make. Easily one of the decade's styling landmarks, the '61 Lincoln was instantly acclaimed so by no less than the prestigious Industrial Design Institute. A problem with the Lincoln's short (by Sixties luxury-car standards)123-inch wheelbase was that it was hard to exit the rear seat without kicking the door. That was solved by hinging the rear doors at the rear. The excellent Continental design didn't require regular styling updates; however, a subtle facelift was executed for 1966, with production continuing through 1969. A 1968 model is shown.

Former race car driver Carroll Shelby dropped a Ford V-8 into an AC to create the lightning-quick Shelby Cobra. The AC was a lightweight English sports car with a tubular frame and four-wheel-independent suspension. The first Cobras had a 260-cid V-8, that was later increased 289 cid. A big 427 V-8 became available in 1965. The 427 was conservatively rated at 390 horsepower, although race versions could provide up to 480 hp. The 427 Cobra was brutally fast with 0-60 mph accomplished in 4.2 seconds. The Cobra was also brutal to control and required a skillful driver to achieve its full potential. Federal regulations killed the Cobra after 1967. A 1965 Shelby Cobra 427 is shown.

The Aston Martin DB5 was a finely built English sports car powered by a 282-horsepower, 4.0-liter dual-overhead-cam six. Top speed was 140 mph, plus there was 325-hp Vantage version that was faster still. The DB5 gained fame in the 1964 James Bond movie *Goldfinger*, where it was fitted with such gadgets as an ejector seat, machine guns hidden in the front fenders, wheel-hub-mounted tire slashers, smoke screen, and retractable rear bulletproof shield. The DB5 was built from 1963 through 1965.

Chevrolet's second-generation Corvette was the 1963 Sting Ray. GM design boss Bill Mitchell's 1959 Stingray Special racer inspired the swoopy styling, and for the first time, a stylish close coupe joined the convertible. The coupe had a distinctive split rear window only in '63, and both bodies were made of fiberglass. Underneath there was an all-new chassis with Corvette's firs independent rear suspension. Power came from Chevy's proven 327-cubic-inch V-8 in several states of tune. Base horsepower was 250 with a four-barrel carburetor, and the top fuel-injecte

Many consider the Jeep Wagoneer the first luxury sport utility vehicle. When introduced for the 1963 model year, the Wagoneer was lower and more car-like than the previous Jeep Station Wagon. Although it had good ground clearance, step-in height wasn't much higher than that of a car. The first automatic transmission offered in a four-wheel-drive vehicle further broadened its appeal. The station-wagon-like styling aged well and the last Wagoneer was sold during 1992.

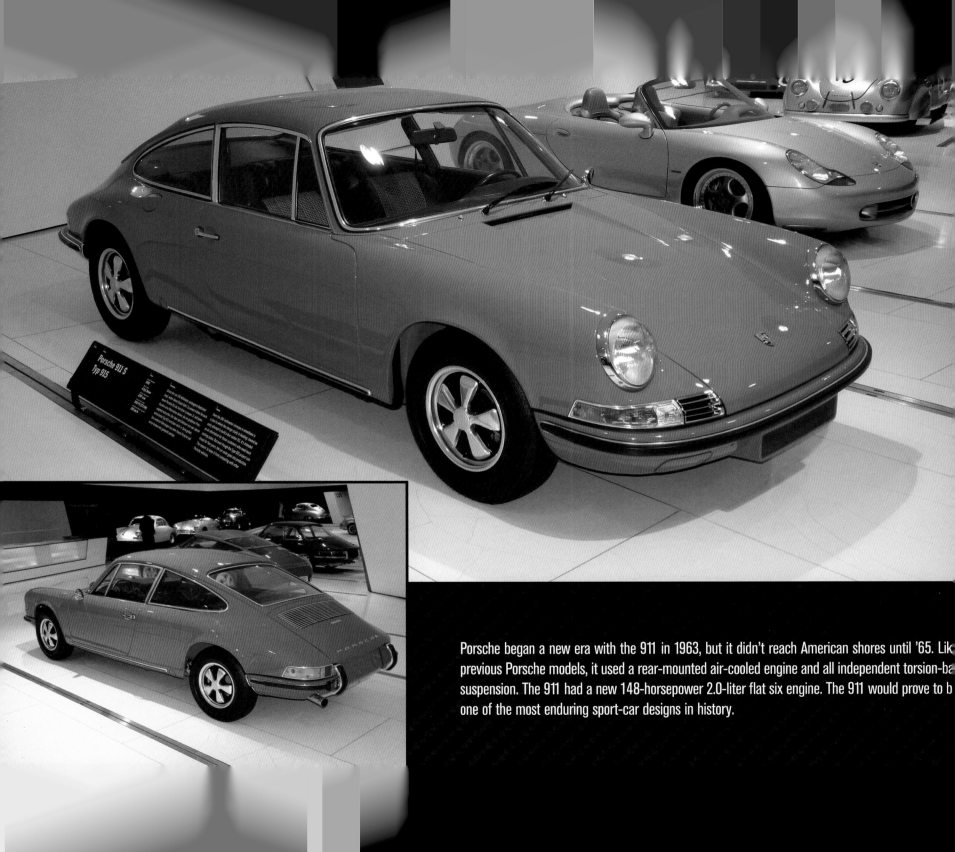

Porsche began a new era with the 911 in 1963, but it didn't reach American shores until '65. Like previous Porsche models, it used a rear-mounted air-cooled engine and all independent torsion-ba suspension. The 911 had a new 148-horsepower 2.0-liter flat six engine. The 911 would prove to b one of the most enduring sport-car designs in history.

Rebuffed when it tried to buy Ferrari, Ford created the GT40 to exact revenge in international long-distance racing. The basic midengined design originated in Britain, but was heavily reworked by Carroll Shelby and other Americans after a troubled 1964 debut. Ford reached a pinnacle in 1966 with smashing 1-2-3 finishes at Le Mans and Daytona. The GT40 went on to win at Le Mans in 1967-69. Its Ford V-8s ranged from 289 to 427 cid with 485 horsepower for the 427. The GT40 could reach 215 mph. Ford built 130 racing GT40s and 31 street cars.

Many consider the 1964 Pontiac Tempest GTO the first "muscle car," a midsize car with a big, high-powered V-8. To create the GTO, Pontiac sidestepped GM's prohibition on intermediate-sized cars having engines over 330 cid. In a ploy that didn't require corporate approval, Pontiac made its 325/348-horsepower 389-cid V-8 part of a $296 option package for the new Tempest. In top trim, a GTO could run 0-60 mph in 6.5 seconds and handle the quarter mile in under 15 seconds at nearly 100 mph. The GTO launched the muscle car era.

The Ford Mustang debuted on April 17, 1964 at the New York World's Fair. Though based on humble mechanicals from Ford's Falcon compact, the sporty Mustang proved extremely popular. Originally offered as a two-door notchback hardtop or convertible, a 2+2 fastback coupe soon joined them as a third body style. Mustang was the first "pony car," generally defined as a reasonably priced sporty small car with a long hood, short deck, and bucket-seat interior. Prices started at $2372, and the extensive options list meant almost anybody could find a Mustang

Some consider the 1967 Lamborghini Miura the first "supercar." The Miura broke with convention by placing its 350-horsepower V-12 midship. By the Seventies, most exotic sports cars were midengined. By 1971, the Miura SV had a 385-hp engine and was capable of 0-60 mph in 5.8 seconds with a top speed of 180 mph. The last Miura was sold in early 1973.

In 1968, the BMW 2002 cemented BMW's reputation for building sporty European coupes. The lightweight coupe had a 2.0-liter four-cylinder that developed 100 horsepower in base carbureted form or 125 hp in the fuel-injected tii models. In 1973, a turbocharged version with 170 hp was added. The 2002 had sports car handling and performance, but it also had a usable back seat. The 2002 was sold through 1976 and was replaced by the even more successful BMW 3 Series.

The 1968 Dodge Charger is one of the most iconic cars of the Muscle Era. In these cars, Dodge achieved a fine combination of classic lines and outstanding performance. The top '68 was the R/T (Road/Track), which produced 375 horsepower with Dodge's 440 Magnum V-8, or a thumping 425 hp with optional 426-cid Hemi. These cars delivered serious performance: 6.5 seconds 0-60 mph with the 440, and mid-five runs with the Hemi. R/Ts equipped with the 440 topped out at 113 mph, while the Hemi versions didn't quit until 142-156 mph. The restyled 1971 Charger that followed placed more emphasis on luxury than performance, making the classic 1968-70 Chargers the more desirable.

Many consider the 1968 Ferrari 365 GTB/4 (which the press dubbed Daytona) the greatest of the classic front-engine, two-seat production Ferraris. The 4.4-liter V-12 produced 352 horsepower and was capable of 174 mph. Initially offered only as a fastback coupe, a convertible Daytona was added for 1969. The Daytona's excellent handling and performance, combined with beautiful styling, has made the Daytona one of the most valuable and collectible Ferraris.

Plymouth found a ready market when it introduced its budget-priced muscle car, the Road Runner, in 1968. The Road Runner left out the creature comforts, but included a standard 335-horsepower, 383-cid V-8, four-speed manual transmission, and heavy-duty suspension. A 425-hp Hemi V-8 was optional. Properly equipped, a Road Runner could run the quarter-mile in 13.5 seconds at 105 mph. Road Runner was serious about performance, but had a whimsical name, cartoon decals, and a "Beep-Beep" horn courtesy of a licensing deal with Warner Bros.

The 1969 Jaguar XJ set a new standard for European luxury sedans. It was quiet with an incredibly smooth ride, yet it also had excellent handling. The XJ's styling was so successful that Jaguar used variations of the theme through 2009. Jaguar's familiar dohc six was joined by a V-12 for 1972. The original design was in production through 1992 and Jaguar's current flagship sedan is still badged XJ.

In the 1960s Datsun offered a series of four-cylinder powered sports cars. Those roadsters were replaced with the 1970 Datsun 240Z, and it proved an instant success. The sleek hatchback had scooped headlights, a mile long hood, and a racy fastback roofline. The well-equipped interior had bucket seats for two. Power came from a 2.4-liter OHC inline six good for 150 horsepower mated to a 4-speed manual transmission. Other highlights included four-wheel independent suspension and unibody construction. The car's performance approached that of European rivals selling for nearly double the 240Z's $3526 starting price. Comfort items like air conditioning and an automatic transmission were not available.

The 1970 Land Rover Range Rover started the SUV-as-status-symbol trend. The Range Rover was designed to be more comfortable and capable on-road than the original Land Rover. Its aluminum V-8 began as a Buick design, but production tooling was purchased by Rover in the late Sixties. Top speed was around 100 mph. Coil springs on all four corners ensured a comfortable ride. The off-road abilities weren't neglected and the Range Rover could go almost anywhere. Rover thought the Range Rover would sell mostly to prosperous farmers and veterinarians, but these luxury SUVs soon were a common sight in London and other cities.

The Pontiac Firebird's (and related Chevrolet Camaro) second generation had fresh styling with a Ferrari GTO influence. Performance took a dive in the Seventies, but the Pontiac Firebird, with its available big V8s, reasonable size, and relatively nimble handling, was a bright spot in a dark age. A prime example was the 1977 Trans Am used in the film *Smokey and the Bandit*. The second-generation Firebird was produced through 1981.

The fun to drive and reliable 1973 Honda Civic brought the front-wheel-drive economy car into the American mainstream. Its timing couldn't have been better with the Oil Embargo hitting not long after the Civic's introduction. Honda claimed up to 30 mpg and couldn't build cars fast enough. For 1975 Honda introduced the CVCC (Compound Vortex Controlled Combustion) engine that efficiently met tightening emissions standards without a catalytic converter.

The Lamborghini Countach was one of the wildest supercars ever built and appeared on thousands of posters and calendars. Scissor doors that opened up and forward were a unique feature. Production began in late 1973 and ended in 1990. The final Countach had a 455-horsepower V-12 and had a top speed of 183 mph. The factory claimed 0-60 mph in 4.7 seconds with a quarter-mile time of 12.9 seconds.

In 1974 Volkswagen made a historic turn from air-cooled rear-mounted engines to water-cooled front engines and front-wheel drive for the compact Golf. The Golf arrived in America in 1975 as the VW Rabbit. In 1976, Europeans got a GTI version of the Golf with a more powerful engine and sport suspension. The "hot hatch" segment was born and its combination of sporty moves and family-car practicality proved popular. Americans wouldn't get a Rabbit GTI until 1983 and '84 was the last year of the first-generation GTI.

Even before the 1973 Oil Embargo, General Motors had decided that its full-sized cars were too big. Development of trimmer cars was already in progress when the energy crisis made downsizing imperative. The 1977 full-sized Impala was 10 inches shorter and more than 600 pounds lighter than the 1976 model, yet interior room remained nearly the same. New styling featured crisp lines that GM styling chief, Bill Mitchell, called the "sheer look." GM's first downsizing was a success with Chevy's big-car sales increasing 56.1 percent over the previous year. The 1977 downsizing proved that Americans would accept smaller cars.

1980 AMC EAGLE

The AMC Eagle was a clever idea from a gutsy company in dire straits. AMC's Jeep division combined its four-wheel-drive expertise with AMC's compact Concord car to create a forerunner of today's crossover SUV. The Eagle merged the comfort and refinement of a car with the security of an SUV's four-wheel drive. A raised ride height and lower body cladding gave the Eagle a rugged look–a trend that continues today. Still, the Eagle couldn't save AMC and the last examples were built under Chrysler ownership as 1988 models.

can be argued that the '82 Honda Accord changed the way that Americans thought about Japanese cars. By this time many car shoppers had heard good things about Honda, bu
he cars were still a little too small, a little too modestly powered, and a little too, well, Japanese-looking. That all changed for 1982. All new that year, Accord grew up before shoppers
ves. The car now stood taller, boasted substantial-looking creased lines, and offered a decent increase in horsepower and torque. Also worth noting, 1982 was the first year for U.S.

Ford, along with most American cars, had boxy styling in the early Eightie
Ford had dabbled with an aero look for the 1979 Mustang, but it was with th
redesigned 1983 Thunderbird that Ford committed to aerodynamic stylin
The "Aero Bird" not only looked streamlined, it was aerodynamic with a 0.3
coefficient of drag that was the lowest of any of the Big Three's two-do
cars. The slippery design was a boon to Ford in NASCAR racing. Subseque
Ford designs were smooth and rounded and the industry followed.

1984 DODGE CARAVAN

The minivan idea had been kicking around for decades, but either it was a concept that never made it to production or it was not quite mainstream, such as the Volkswagen bus. Chrysler Corporation, under the leadership of Lee Iacocca, had the guts to launch the minivan as a 1984 model. Full-sized vans were too tall for most garages and were trucklike to drive. The Dodge Caravan, along with the similar Plymouth Voyager, combined the expansive interior of a van with a front-drive sedan platform. The result was carlike to drive and had a low step-in height, yet could hold up to eight passengers and luggage. A new market was created, and school parking lots would soon be filled with minivans.

1986 FORD TAURUS

The American midsize sedan segment was one of the most conservative, yet for 1986, Ford introduced its daring Taurus sedan and wagon. Many of the Taurus design team had experience with Ford of Europe and Taurus had European style and driving dynamics. Ford had success with its aerodynamic 1983 Thunderbird and the Taurus followed its design lead. Ford's gamble paid off and the Taurus was one of the company's most successful products. The midsize sedan market was forever changed.

Toyota introduced its upmarket Lexus brand for 1990. The LS 400 challenged the Mercedes-Benz S-Class and other European luxury sedans, but for significantly less money. The LS was incredibly quiet and had a comfortable ride. It was also extremely well built and reliable. The luxury-car market changed forever with the entry of Lexus.

1990 MAZDA MIATA MX-5

The Mazda Miata was a timeless reinterpretation of the classic British/Italian sports car for the Nineties. The Miata was an affordable, fully open, volume sports car that introduced a new generation to the joys of sports cars. The first-generation Miata had a 1.6-liter twin-cam four with 116 horsepower. With only 2182 pounds to move, performance, while not blistering, was entertaining. With quick reflexes and good grip, the Miata was a blast to drive.

THEATER
ENTRANCE

Before the Ford Explorer arrived on the scene for the 1991 model year, shoppers looking for family-hauling flexibility had several choices: sedan, station wagon, minivan, or full-size van. The Explorer changed all of that. Prior to the Explorer, small SUVs were relatively cramped inside and crude in nature. Ford fashioned the Explorer with an eye towards refinement and family-friendly passenger and cargo space. Today, SUVs dominate the market and the Explorer was responsible for the shift to SUVs as mainstream transportation.

The Dodge Viper was the spiritual successor of the Shelby Cobra. Like the Cobra, the Viper wasn't high-tech or refined. It was an unapologetic celebration of American brute horsepower unencumbered by gadgetry or creature comforts. The 8.0-liter V-10 was rated at 400 horsepower with 465 lb-ft of torque. It was loud and uncomfortable, but it was also brutally fast and gorgeous. Dodge claimed the Viper could accelerate 0-60 mph in 4.5 seconds and cover the quarter mile in 12.9 seconds at 113 mph. The first-generation Viper ended production in 2002.

As SUVs became more popular in the Nineties, Jeep decided to bring out a larger, more upmarket version of its Cherokee for 1993. The Grand Cherokee had a more carlike ride than other SUVs of the time and yet it still retained the off-road ability expected of a Jeep. Power was provided by an 190-horsepower inline six or a 220-hp V-8. The Grand Cherokee proved that there were plenty of buyers for luxury SUVs and top end of the sport ute market continued to expand.

1994 MCLAREN F1

Drawing on its multiple Formula 1, CanAm, and Indianapolis victories, England's McLaren organization set about creating its first road car. The McLaren F1 was on the road by 1994 and in the winner's circle at Le Mans in 1995. Scissor-type doors provided access to a leather interior with an unusual "1+2" layout: a form-fitting driver seat was centrally located, with passenger seats slightly aft on both sides. A BMW-designed 6.1-liter V-12 was mounted amidships and packed 627 horsepower. Price and performance were equally stratospheric: $810,000, 0-60 mph in 3.2 seconds, 11.1-second quarter-mile times, and a 231-mph top speed. When production ceased in 1997, only 100 cars (including competition versions) had been built.

Toyota started the compact, crossover SUV or "cute ute" trend with the RAV4. The RAV4 was introduced for the Japanese and European markets in 1994 and reached North America in 1996. There had been other small SUVs before, but the RAV4 was based on the Corolla car platform. The RAV4 offered SUV benefits with carlike ride and handling. Its 120-horsepower four-cylinder wasn't powerful, but it delivered good fuel economy. The RAV4 proved to be just the vehicle that many were looking for.

By the final decade of the 20th century, it was becoming clear that electric cars would be part of the future of transportation. General Motors embarked on a billion-dollar program to build an electric car. The production EV1 closely resembled the Impact concept car (shown) that debuted at the 1990 LA Auto Show. In order to maximize range and efficiency, the EV1 was a two-seater built of lightweight materials and with a low aerodynamic drag coefficient of 0.19. Introduced for 1997 with lead-acid batteries, the EV1 had a range of 50 to 70 miles. In 1999, optional nickel-metal hydride batteries increased the range to 100-140 miles. GM chose to lease, not sell, the experimental EV1 and later took possession of all the cars rather than face liability risks and the expense of supplying parts for a discontinued model. Many EV1 owners were quite enthusiastic about their cars and didn't want to give them up—especially since most were scrapped. The 2006 documentary film *Who Killed the Electric Car?* exaggerated the death of the electric car. There are now several electric cars on the market and GM introduced the electric Chevrolet Bolt EV for 2017.

Excluding pickup trucks, the single largest segment of the American auto market today is crossover. Crossovers are generally similar in design to truck-based SUVs, but are engineered on carlike architecture, allowing them to be lighter, more space-efficient, and often less costly than SUVs. One of the earliest vehicles to be described as a luxury crossover was the 1999 Lexus RX 300. The RX showed that a vehicle could have the space, high seating position, and rugged appeal of an SUV, but with greater comfort and fuel economy.

The Toyota Prius (along with the less practical Honda Insight two-seater) helped introduce Americans to the concept of battery-assisted propulsion. The gas-electric hybrid drivetrain significantly reduced fuel consumption and emissions, and soon the environmentally conscious adopted the Prius as a mascot. Many others discovered the Prius was a practical car that was economical to operate. The first-generation Prius introduced the world to hybrids, although it was the second generation, that debuted for 2004, that normalized the technology and sold in impressive volume.

Under Volkswagen control, the latest revival of the storied Bugatti name was free of the financial limitations that killed a 1990s rebirth effort. Bugatti's twenty-first century renaissance began with the Veyron and its promised 1001-horsepower V-16. Federalized models actually delivered 987 hp, roughly double Viper's power output. Production began for 2005, and was limited to 50 vehicles annually. Veyron production ended in 2015.

Ford's iconic Mustang was riding on a platform that had been last redesigned for 1979 when the 2005 Mustang debuted. Styling echoed Mustangs of the past, yet was fresh and modern. The base engine was a 210 horsepower V-6 and a 300-hp V-8 powered GTs. Ford revived the Shelby GT500 in 2007 with a 500-hp version of the Mustang. The redesigned Mustang was better in almost every way compared to the car it replaced and proved that the "pony car" wasn't dead.

While established car companies seemingly sat on the sidelines, convinced that electric vehicles (EVs) had to be small, affordable, and practical, California-based Tesla reached wealthy early adopters with a car that was good looking, exciting to drive, and packed with counterculture cachet. Properly equipped, a Model S would travel 300 miles on a charge and zipped to 60 mph in three seconds. The Model S changed countless minds regarding the potential of battery-powered vehicles and set the stage for other makes to enter the electric-car field.

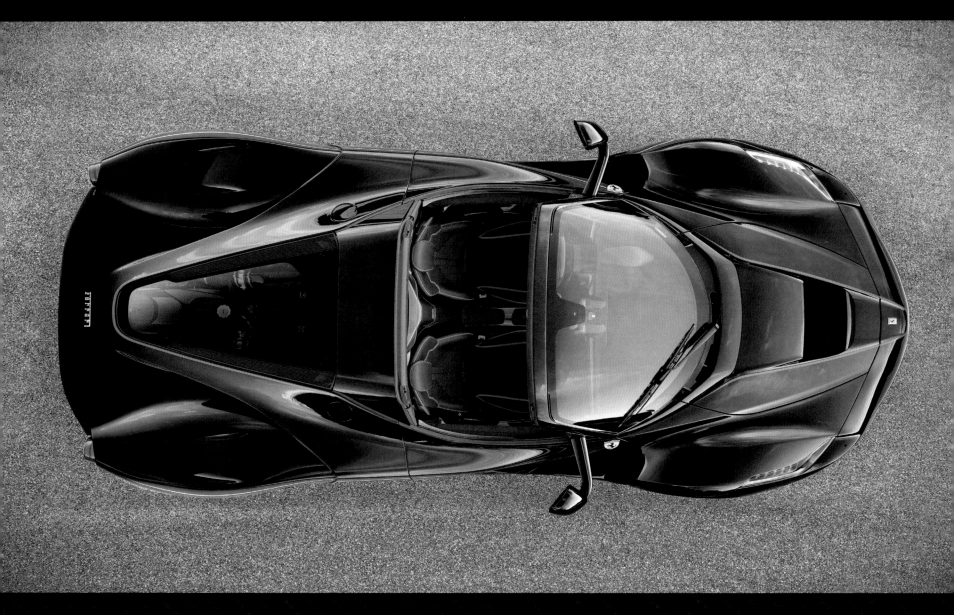

the new millennium, even supercars have to consider the environment. Ferrari would be the last make expected to sell a hybrid, but the LaFerrari was no ordinary hybrid—it combined 88-horsepower V-12 with a 161-hp electric motor for a total of 949 hp. Introduced for 2013, the LaFerrari hybrid was even faster than Ferrari's celebrated 2003-04 Enzo model—it coul ocket 0-60 mph in less than three seconds and hit a top speed of 217 mph. The LaFerrari's price tag was a cool $1.4 million, but Ferrari had no trouble selling 500 coupes, as well as 21

BMW considered the idea of an exotic sports car with a high-tech, eco-conscious focus. The i8 launched as a 2014 model, with unorthodox styling that covered an equally unconventional plug-in hybrid powertrain. The i8's gas-electric powertrain paired a turbocharged 1.5-liter 3-cylinder engine rated at 228 horsepower with a BMW-made electric motor that was good for 129 hp. Combined output was 357 hp and 420 lb-ft of torque. The gasoline engine drove the rear wheels and the electric motor sent its power to the front wheels. BMW quoted the i8's 0-60 mph time at 4.2 seconds and the EPA's gas-electric mileage estimate was 76 MPGe in combined city/highway driving. BMW added several updates for the 2019 i8, including the addition of a roadster.

The SRT Hellcat was a complete monster that was arguably defined by one thing—a 707-horsepower supercharged 6.2-liter Hemi V-8. At the time, the Hellcat had the most horsepower of any American car. Only foreign exotics, costing several times the Hellcat's $59,995 base price, had more power. Dodge said the Hellcat was the most powerful muscle car ever. In common with muscle cars of the golden age, the Hellcat was made for the drag strip. The Hellcat could lay down a National Hot Rod Association-certified quarter-mile run of 11.2 seconds with drag radial tires.

The 2015 Mercedes-Benz F 015 Luxury in Motion concept vehicle was Mercedes' prediction of transportation in the year 2030 when autonomous driving would be commonplace. The Luxury in Motion's front seats could swivel around to aid conversation with the rear passengers. Six screens provided information about the vehicle and a connection with the outside world. Unlike many concept vehicles that are inoperable, the Luxury in Motion was powered by hydrogen fuel cell that supplied current for two electric motors.

The 2017 Chevrolet Bolt EV was a game changer in the world of electric vehicles. It was a popularly-priced electric that had more than double the range (an estimated 238 miles) of mos[t] other electric cars at the time. (The Tesla Model S also had 200-mile-plus range, but it started at about $60,000.) The Bolt, in spite of its subcompact exterior size, had plenty of room for fou[r] passengers and their luggage. It was also fun to drive with peppy acceleration and sporty handling. For many, the Bolt was the first practical alternative to the gas-powered car.

The 2019 Jaguar I-Pace was the first all-electric, all-wheel drive crossover SUV from an established manufacturer and many more makes were expected to follow Jaguar's lead. The I-Pace combined two trends: the rise of pure electric vehicles and the shift from sedans to SUVs. The I-Pace had an EPA-estimated driving range of 234 miles and much quicker acceleration than expected for an all-electric vehicle: Jaguar claimed a 4.5-second 0-60-mph time.

The late Zora Arkus-Duntov was the godfather of Chevrolet Corvette during its first three decades and pushed for a midengined 'Vette in the Seventies. The Aerovette prototype came close reaching production for 1980, but Chevrolet decided to continue with the conventional front-engine Corvette instead. Duntov's dream of a midengined Corvette was finally fulfilled for 2020 he mid-engine layout has long the norm for exotic supercars, now Corvette joins the club. Chevy claims the eighth-generation Corvette will go 0-60 mph in less than three seconds and has top speed of 194. In spite of its exotic-car specs, the new Corvette started at a reasonable $59,995.